Spiritual Discernment

The Guide to Trusting in the Direction of God

Angela Grace

Spiritual Discernment

Spiritual Discernment is a complete guide to hearing God in your life This book covers matters ranging from your life's purpose to everyday things. Angela Grace uses an approachable, simple to understand language that everyone, believers and nonbelievers, can understand and apply to their lives. She demystifies the often misunderstood gift of discernment and provides simple to follow habits that will help grow this spectacular gift. In the following chapters we will discuss these topics:

How do I hear God?

How can I tell it is God?

What should I do with my life?

Why does purpose matter?

How can I trust God with my life?

What is the spiritual world?

How can I tell between good spirits from bad spirits?

How do I live with wisdom?

As well as many other topics. Join Angela Grace on this journey of self-discovery and growth towards spiritual enlightenment.

Download the Audio Version of This Book FREE

This book is best enjoyed in its audio format! If you love listening to audio books on-the-go, I have great news for you. You can download the audio book version of this book for **FREE** just by signing up for a **FREE** 30-day audible trial! See below for more details!

Audible trial benefits

As an audible customer, you'll receive the below benefits with you 30-day free trial:

- Free audible copy of this book

- After the trial, you will get 1 credit each month to use on any audiobook

- Your credits automatically roll over to the next month if you don't use them

- Choose from over 400,000 titles

- Listen anywhere with the audible app across multiple devices

- Make easy, no hassle exchanges of any audiobook you don't love

- Keep your audiobooks forever, even if you cancel your membership

- And much more

Go to the links below to get started

FOR AUDIBLE US

bit.ly/spiritualdiscernmentlisten

FOR AUDIBLE UK

bit.ly/spiritualdiscernmentlistenuk

Bonus!

Wouldn't it be nice to have even more motivation, inspiration and courage on your spiritual path? As a sincere "Thank you" from the bottom of my heart, i've given you access to a FREE powerful 10 minute guided gratitude meditation below. Gratitude is the key to all of your life's abundance, joy, and manifests a wealth of love and light. Practicing the meditation below each day has enriched my life immensely, I just know it will do the same for you.

Are You Searching For The Guidance of God's Higher Power?

- Connect To His Light Easily Through The Power of Gratitude

- Clear The Haze of Uncertainty From Your Life Path

- Discern More Easily Between Bad Spirits & Good

Go To This Link For Your FREE 10 Min Guided Meditation Mp3

bit.ly/spiritualdiscernmentmp3

This meditation often helped me immensely when his exact path for me was not always overtly clear. Resting in gratitude for the beauty I already had in my life cleared the haze & created more of the same. I know these words will help guide you towards your destiny with courage and determination!

Please Leave a Review

From the bottom of my heart, thank you for reading my book. I truly hope that it helps you on your spiritual journey and to live a more empowered and happy life. If it does help you, then I'd like to ask you for a favor. Would you be kind enough to leave an honest review for this book on Amazon? It'd be greatly appreciated and will likely impact the lives of other spiritual seekers across the globe, giving them hope and power.

I read **EVERY** review I receive & each one helps me to become a better spiritual teacher so that I can serve you better.

Thank you and good luck!

Angela Grace

© Copyright 2020 - All rights reserved.

The content contained within this book may not be reproduced, duplicated or transmitted without direct written permission from the author or the publisher.

Under no circumstances will any blame or legal responsibility be held against the publisher, or author, for any damages, reparation, or monetary loss due to the information contained within this book, either directly or indirectly.

Legal Notice:

This book is copyright protected. It is only for personal use. You cannot amend, distribute, sell, use, quote or paraphrase any part, or the content within this book, without the consent of the author or publisher.

Disclaimer Notice:

Please note the information contained within this document is for educational and entertainment purposes only. All effort has been executed to present accurate, up to date, reliable, complete information. No warranties of any kind are declared or implied. Readers acknowledge that the author is not engaged in the rendering of legal, financial, medical or professional advice. The content within this book has been derived from various sources. Please consult a licensed professional before attempting any techniques outlined in this book.

By reading this document, the reader agrees that under no circumstances is the author responsible for any losses, direct or indirect, that are incurred as a result of the use of the information contained within this document, including, but not limited to, errors, omissions, or inaccuracies.

Table of Contents

Spiritual Discernment ii
Bonus! v
Table of Contents ix
Introduction 1
Chapter 1 8
Hearing God 8
    How Can I Tell? 13
    Now What? 18
Chapter 2 25
Purpose 25
    Why Does It Matter? 26
    Here's How You Know 28
    What You Should Do Before Listening 31
Chapter 3 34
Day to Day 34
    The Small Things Matter 34
    How to Listen 37
Chapter 4 41
Light of Darkness 41
    Nature of Spirits 41
    Here's How You Know 43
    Separate Bad Things from Evil 48
    People Under the Influence of Spirits 50
Chapter 5 53

Wisdom 53
    What It Is 53
    God's Wisdom in Action 54
Conclusion 56
Bonus! 58

Introduction

"But the Helper, the Holy Spirit, whom the Father will send in my name, he will teach you all things and bring to your remembrance all that I have said to you" **- John 14:26, (English Standard Version)**

Here is something you probably know, but I am going to tell it to you anyway. Perhaps you don't know this or haven't thought about it. Regardless I am going to be telling you about it. Maybe the way I say it to you will help you realize and appreciate something about the world that you never have before.

Look around you. What do you see? Pictures are moving about on the screen. You hear the chirp of the birds outside. Maybe you live in the city, where all you hear is the roar of the city and the fervor of activity, not easy to pierce through with your ears or isolate. How does this book feel in your hands, is it smooth? If you are reading this on a device, how does it feel? Is the device solid and sturdy in your hands, are the buttons on the screen smooth to your touch? Is it heavy or surprisingly light for its size? How about the chair you are sitting in, is it comfortable? How about those sensations in your body, the niggle in your left knee, the way your skin stretches and contracts as you move?

This is all exciting and nice, and you might even say that it is real as opposed to something that is a dream or fictional. Here is the strange part about all of this, it is a real-time simulation being run by your brain. These feelings, perceptions, sights, and stuff you hear. This is not to say that there aren't things like tables, chairs, and bodies that exist in the world; there are objects in the world that serve these purposes and present themselves that way. The point I want you to realize is that your brain is in a black box. It gets inputs from your senses, and using a bunch of techniques, it simulates a world for you: taste, touch, sight, internal sensations, and much more. But we know, both from what we know about science and our experiences, that the way we perceive the world isn't exactly how the world is. We have technologies in our life that exploit the fact that our brains are blind to a lot that is out there. Consider the TV in your living room or any screen for that matter. When you look at it, you see people on the screen talking; when you swipe up the page, it scrolls. But you do realize this is an illusion, but like any other illusions in works by exploiting how our brain interprets visual input to build a world. It is a type of optical illusion, as you know.

The point I am making is that the world is not as it seems. We can't live a wholesome life that is tuned with nature and the world by our own wits or experience. Most of the things that happen in the universe, and I mean universe as absolutely everything that exists, including matter, are not in our direct experience or observation. They are invisible to us. And many of these things that are invisible to us have real effects on us. They have implications for our lives here on earth. Just because something is vast and far away, just because you are unable to see something doesn't mean it can't hurt you or embolden you. It doesn't make it not exist or matter less. If your goal is to live a life that is genuinely fulfilling, successful, and in harmony with the ultimate existence, it would make sense to see beyond the world that has been pulled over your eyes by the limits of your own perceptions, experience, and nature.

A person who does not see beyond their immediate reality or experience is like a person stumbling in the dark. They have no insight or perception of how their decisions reverberate beyond what they can see. Since people are more than their direct experience, they have a soul. They might also be making decisions that harm the soul in the long term.

How do you turn that around, though? How do you see beyond your immediate, small reality and make decisions that are wise beyond your direct experience? You have to learn to be spiritually aware and alert. To do that you will need some help, the best help, guidance, you get is from God. Well, you might think I am a little biased, going for God right off the bat. What if there is some other spirit, Cthulhu or Leviathan, who is more equipped to help you? Before we get into it, let's talk about what spirits are. Many people think of spirits as existing separate from or beyond physical reality. As we have seen, physical reality, or the world as we experience it, is a tiny slither of what is actually out there. Spirits are being, which are residents of this fuller reality. They see much more than the world than us. By us, I mean most of us because we have souls; at the fundamental level, we are souls. But some spirits are more conscious of others, they know more, see more and can do more than others. This is just like here in the real world. Some people are just more capable than other people.

Now, imagine if the entire world was one country. The most influential person in that country we would call the President. The word God describes something like that. It is a title. God is not the name of God. God has an actual name. Just like how your President's name isn't President. But with God, there is another element that makes them the best guy to listen to. They made everything that exists. They are the ultimate architects. So, they know everything about their existence because it is their design. That is why we say God is all-knowing; he literally is. God didn't have an algorithm to make him the universe; he designed it all. Not only does he know all, but he must also be super-intelligent. More intelligent than anything that could exist, because any intelligence that exists in the universe exists as a result of his design, meaning it is his design. So, God is your guy if you want to have the best life. He knows best because he is the best that can ever be.

There is a problem, though. This is why we have this book right here. There is an infinite number of other spirits who try to sell you the same services. Sometimes, often, it is difficult to know which one is God and which one isn't. This is because of two things. One is that we have spiritually neglected ourselves. We are spiritually malnourished, so to speak. So, we are terrible at acting in the spiritual world because of this.

The second problem is that there are forces out there that are hell-bent of destroying us or thwarting our attempts to make a connection with God. There is simply too much noise. Put simply, it takes some effort, maintained effort to hear God. Some people might be quick to ask why.

My response is to ask why it should be otherwise? We like the people we are in relationships with because it is a two-way street. Relationships are built on the idea that both parties are making an effort to build something together. God is already making an effort; you are not living up to your part of the bargain. If you don't believe me that God talks to us all the time, I will give one proof that is difficult to dispute.

Think back to when you were a child and your mother baked those lovely cookies you like. She put them in a jar, told you not to have any until she gives them to you. Maybe she told you should ask first. But three or five cookies in the morning wasn't enough for you. You wanted more. It is not your fault. They were very delicious cookies. Your mouth is watering just thinking about them. Side note: Maybe you should call your mom and tell her to bake you some this instant. Be kind, though. Anyway, back to our story. You know what you did next. You went and stole some. Maybe one here and there, but soon it became ten or twenty, and you got caught. Right? But you probably remember, despite the thrill of stealing, that bad feeling in your chest or that voice in the back of your head telling you that you shouldn't do it. You knew right then that what you were doing was wrong, and there was a voice that told you it was. We call this voice a conscience; our conscience is one of the purest ways God talks to us.

But as you know, this channel can get hijacked by other influences and spirits, but when you were a kid, that probably hadn't happened yet. And God probably talked to you more often, not only when you were doing bad things, but when you were playing too. Do you remember that feeling of a presence? Of being watched over, observed, how you would sometimes talk to yourself, or to something, but you weren't quite sure what? The thing that is not your imaginary friend? Just thinking about it.

But you came to this book because, in a sense, you have lost that at a point in your life when you need more of it. One of the reasons that spirits don't spend as much effort binding kids; it is because kids make fewer decisions. They have fewer responsibilities. There the more choices you have, the more power you have, and the more useful you are as a person. This is not saying children are less important. They are, it may be part of the reason that they attack parents and adults because confused adults can confuse the children too. Since you make more decisions and your decisions echo across generations, you need God now more than ever. So, picking up this book has been one of the most clever decisions you have ever made. Perhaps God himself has guided you here.

In this book, I will talk about what it takes to hear God, how do you tell it is God. I will talk about finding your purpose and why that matters. We will explore how God talks to us day by day and how we can use that to grow in faith. The most interesting chat for most of you will be my discussion on discerning good spirits from bad spirits, good intentions, and bad intentions. We will discuss living by scripture and wisdom. This will be a lot of fun. This book is about spiritual discernment, and so far, I have said a lot about hearing God. This is because as much as discernment is having great spiritual perception, much of it grows from and is informed by two-way communication with God. So, this discussion necessitates a discussion on hearing God, listening to God, and also ways to distinguish between different voices, intentions, and spirits.

Chapter 1

Hearing God

At its most basic, God talks to us through the spirit. This is helpful because the spirit is always around us and within us. He speaks in different ways and there are many ways God uses the spirit to talk to us. God speaks to us differently, depending on who we are, where we are, and what our trajectory in life is. He talks to each individual differently, but it is all to serve one ultimate goal: achieve great intimacy and bring about his kingdom. While I can't provide a set of instructions on how you can begin to hear God in your life, I can tell you there are set ways that God does communicate. Still, the nature in which he uses these ways will differ with each person. There will be great overlaps, though.

In these chapters I will go over the readily available ways that God communicates with us, some are so used to these ways that they no longer think of it as something out of the ordinary. The most common being the conscience; this is like a built-in mechanism that connects God to each person. The only problem is this mechanism can become corrupted. We know this because there are people who disagree strongly on things that should be the same for all. These worldviews can alter our conscience.

Substitute the word 'worldview' here for 'information.' A worldview consists of a set of concepts that relate to each other in a complex manner. Imagine you are given land. The land is lush, and a lot will grow there so you decide to start growing a few crops. Before you can do that, you have to clear what's already growing there. If the information you have is that clearing the field will lead to a high crop yield, established jobs, food for others, and support for your family, clearing the field will feel like the best thing to do.

Now imagine the same situation, but you have a different set of information. For example, you know clearing the field will lead to the town flooding in the summer, causing irreparable damage and possibly loss of life. You might feel bad about clearing the field even if you know it will lead to wealth and support for your family. The information you have, the concepts, can have a great influence on your conscience and decision making. What this illustrates is how easy it is for conscience to be swayed. If your worldview is biblical, your conscience will, for the most part, be aligned with God's desires. But you can't always be sure that somehow, something has muddled your conceptions of the word to lead you astray.

Another way God communicates with us is through intuition. Intuition is most famously called a gut feeling. It can be as simple as feeling uneasy about making a particular decision. Sometimes it is confidence in knowing that you should do something, a type of unexplainable knowledge about a situation that later turns out to be true. Intuition is enigmatic in the sense that it does not appeal to the intellect; it affects and deals with something deeply spiritual about our nature.

"For the Lord gives wisdom; from his mouth comes knowledge and understanding; he stores up sound wisdom for the upright; he is a shield to those who walk in integrity, guarding the paths of justice and watching over the way of his saints. Then you will understand righteousness and justice and equity, every good path; for wisdom will come into your heart, and knowledge will be pleasant to your soul;" - Proverbs 2:6-15

Another way that God communicates is through dreams and visions. God can use them to bring something mysterious to the forefront. To make sense of problems we have been struggling with, to give us a different idea about what's next and so much more. While people may obsess about dream interpretation, often, dreams are clear cut because of language, using imagery and emotions, that we understand.

"For God speaks in one way, and in two, though man does not perceive it. In a dream, in a vision of the night, when deep sleep falls on men, while they slumber on their beds, then he opens the ears of men and terrifies them with warnings, that he may turn man aside from his deed and conceal pride from a man; he keeps back his soul from the pit, his life from perishing by the sword." **- Job 33:14-18**

God also uses other people's counsel to communicate with us. Generally, this is something you will hear from people who have a close relationship with God. For instance, if at church, people say something about you, they see something similar, like that you would make an excellent teacher. That would be a way of God showing you that you have this gift. He has paved the way for you to follow it. This is because if people see or recognize something in you, they ascribe a role for you. While you might face some challenges on a route that is acknowledged within the spiritual circle, you will receive adequate support to reach your goal. An even better sign of this is if people who don't communicate with each other say the same thing about a matter in your life.

> *"The way of a fool is right in his own eyes, but a wise man listens to advice."*
>
> **- Proverbs 12:15**

> *"Where there is no guidance, a people falls, but in an abundance of counselors there is safety."*
>
> **- Proverbs 11:14**

The other way that God communicates with us is through his word. Whether by reading it or through sermons and messages. You will know that God is communicating with you if a message or sermon convicts you. The word *convict* is a perfect way to describe the phenomenon. What it essentially means is that you feel like, at that moment, that the message was meant for you, made for you in mind. Of course, no preacher's message or verse was written specifically with you in mind, but you might be positioned in such a way in life that the message resonates deeply with you.

> *"All Scripture is breathed out by God and profitable for teaching, for reproof, for correction, and for training in righteousness, that the man of God may be competent, equipped for every good work."* **- 2 Timothy 3:16-17**

Another way that God communicates with us is more direct. He speaks to us through the voice in our heads, a still voice that speaks spirit to spirit. This might be the point that some people feel uneasy. Still, if you clear your head, meditate in scripture, and do some of the exercises that we will discuss in this book, you will hear ideas, thoughts and get pictures popping in her head that guide you. This thing isn't just thoughts, they are specific to your questions, and they also come with other confirmations. A confirmation is when God says something, and then something happens in the world that corroborates his will or desires for you.

The less common one, something many would love or even pay to experience, is an audible voice. This is when you hear an actual voice the same way you would hear music from your speaker or someone next to you speak. It happens in a distinctly external way. It can be scary or seem that way as you read this. This is because, in our normal experiences, we don't hear voices coming out of thin air, and when they do, it can mean mental instability. God can use this method, and when he does, you will be filled with a sense of calm, peace, and knowing.

Another way is through intense passion. This can be something like a strong, euphoric feeling that comes out of nowhere and propels you towards something. People generally have these types of experiences during worship when the spirit of the Lord comes upon them and is an overwhelming presence. At that moment, a type of supernatural knowledge comes to you; it is so clear and bright that you can't doubt or mistake it.

"So, whether you eat or drink, or whatever you do, do all to the glory of God."

- 1 Corinthians 10:31

"I can do all things through him who strengthens me." **- Philippians 4:13**

God will employ several methods to communicate with you. Just like you wouldn't only communicate with your parents or friends face-to-face. You use every tool at your disposal to transfer a message and use whatever fits best the scenario at hand. If they are far away, you might raise your voice. If you are in another city, you might call them. If you can't talk, you can text them. And if it has been a long time and you miss them, you might video chat your loved ones. God is the same way, and it will likely be the same message, the one that you need to hear right now. This is another way in which confirmations happen as well: the same messages communicated in different ways

How Can I Tell?

Now you know the ways in which God speaks, how can you tell if it is God? This is a central struggle for all believers. I call it the perpetual ambiguity syndrome. When they get a message from God, they either think the source is not clear or they can't be sure it is God as it is not very clear. I often ask these people what they would need to see to be convinced that it is God speaking to them. They never really have an answer, I guess it's because they sense it is rhetorical. I imagine they would like God to reach down from heaven and talk to them in a mass of blinding light. Perhaps that would be proof enough. But who knows for sure?

We have hinted at ways that God reveals himself and they are worth going over briefly. God confirms the things he tells you. He won't say it one time, to only you and in one way. He will say the same thing in different ways. It is like how your partner might text you not to forget the milk when you already know to get the milk. Maybe you dream about starting a 'GoFundMe' page for your neighbor. Then you hear the same voice popping in your head more as you pray, and even start to feel good about it. A friend might ask you why you don't do something similar for your friend. And then, just like that, you know it God talking to you.

You can tell it is good simply because it is good. God wouldn't tell you to do something that is ultimately destructive to you, your loved ones, or your relationship with him. If it is in line with scripture, and it is good, it advances His word and strengthens your relationship with him, then it is God.

"And Jesus said to him, 'Why do you call me good? No one is good except God alone."

- Mark 10:18

It is here that you often hear about the story of God and Abraham. This story often makes people think that God doesn't always tell us to do things that are good or at least look morally acceptable. If you don't know the story, God tells Abraham to sacrifice his son. Abraham comes close to it, right as he is about to strike his head, God tells him to stop and that Abraham has proven his faith. It seems like a cruel joke. Why would God do something like that? How can God be so cruel? Surely then, God doesn't always ask us to do what is good. He is more than capable of telling us to do things and change his mind at the last minute. This seems to be the picture that many people draw from this specific story in the bible. They hear that story, and they see a God who is capricious and capable of instructing people to do morally reprehensible acts for no reason. And with that description, you might feel better calling this entity a devil instead of God.

The people who think this is are often quick to ask questions like, "If God tells you to kill your neighbor, would you do it?" I am afraid I am going to be a bit morbid for the next few sentences. But this only for the sake of argument. Not saying God would do this, but I think the question is worth examining. If you were in this scenario and a voice came to you and said: "I am the Lord your God and savior, and I command you to kill your neighbor." The first thing to go through your head is probably not "Wow, God is speaking to me," it is somewhere between "I am going insane" and "This must be an evil spirit." This is exactly where your thoughts should be. Why? God is not counter-productive. He works to make things better, not to make them worse. The question to ask yourself is: if I were to go to my neighbor and kill him, how would it make me feel? How would those feelings impact my relationship with God and the community? If the answer to that, from what you know about the world, is overwhelmingly negative, then it isn't God. If it means breaking ties with family, disgracing your church, making it hard for you to trust God's message, and leading to potentially irreversible psychological and emotional damage, this isn't God. He would never ask you to do something that might jeopardize your relationship with him.

Now one can imagine a clever terrorist saying, "Well, God would never do anything to harm you. So, he knows that if you kill this person, it will be very good for you."

But remember what I said. If, from what you know now, at this moment, according to the intelligence you have earned, doing such an action looks like it would damage your relationship with God, the church, your family, and bring about hurt and pain, it is not God. The moment you allow yourself to act on ridiculous, wild impulses or invocations because "the spirit knows better," you are opening yourself up to outside influences. A sign that God is speaking to you is that he will make what he says to you intelligible to your current situation. It won't be a complete mystery. I advise you to apply this criterion in the very serious of circumstances. If God tells you to go have pizza, there would be no need for such a review.

"The Lord is good to all, and his mercy is over all that he has made." -
Psalm 145:9

When you spend time studying and praying on scripture, you get used to the voice of God. God's spirit works with you during those times to illuminate the word and bring insight into your life. When you read the word, and you feel convicted by it, you will know it is God speaking to you. And when you are in doubt, you can rest assured that that message can be confirmed outside of scripture. One of the other benefits that come from reading scripture and immersing yourself in the word is that you spend so much time with God's spirit that you can easily recognize God the next time he communicates with you. Your mind will be filled with his word, and when you look out into the world, it will be shaped in such a way it becomes easy to perceive his ways and actions in the world and to recognize him. This may sound weird, but you have had a similar experience before. The spirit opens up our minds or our spiritual eye in the same way knowledge can change how we see things around us.

For example, as any student of varying subjects will tell you, before learning something new they have to know the world around them is full of unseen features. Not because these invisible things aren't there but because the student's mind has yet to be trained on how to recognize them. Before psychology students begin to study their subject, they start off seeing other people's behavior in two-dimensional ways as either good or bad. They make poor judgments about the motivations of others, the way they act, and might see mental health challenges as personality quirks or even bad behavior.

It's when the student begins to see a world that is even more multifaceted, where things are way more complex and intriguing than they appear at first. They are more ready to look at a situation and behavior and then come up with better judgments about the reason for the behavior and if it is normal. Immersing yourself in the word of God gives you the ability to see more than the world that is in front of you, to recognize patterns, hidden influences, and the significance of events around you.

"Your word is a lamp to my feet and a light to my path." **- Psalm 119:105**

That is why the best way to hear God or prime yourself to easily recognize his ways in your life is by acquainting yourself with his word. This will help you easily discern evil spirits.

To reiterate, God is not destructive. God uses more than one way, and he will confirm what he says and if you immersive yourself in scripture, you readily perceive him in other areas in your life.

Now What?

Now you have a good idea of some of the things you should pay attention to or do if you want to discern God's ways in your life. You know why it's important to read and analyze scripture. That is true, but so far, we have talked about how God talks, and how you can know it is him, but we haven't talked about the ways you can actively listen to him. Most of the time, it is not that God is not talking to us; we just never listen. So, I will talk about ways we can listen to God.

Be Bored

Yes, you heard me right, allow yourself to be bored. People nowadays are so afraid of non-activity that they always preoccupy themselves with some form of digital stimulation. In this age and economy, there is no shortage of things to keep us busy if we don't want to be bored. And boredom is uncomfortable, so we avoid it a lot. When we keep ourselves busy, preoccupied, and entertained, we shut out a lot that God might be saying to us because we are too focused on something else. It's like talking to someone who is texting someone else, they aren't paying attention, and sometimes don't hear you at all. Being busy all the time is what texting someone else while in a conversation is to spirituality.

"But when you pray, go into your room and shut the door and pray to your Father who is in secret. And your Father who sees in secret will reward you." **- Matthew 6:6**

So, I am assuming you go to a place of worship, you read scripture, and you are keen to hear God speak to you. Try this exercise if you want to hear God. Disclaimer: This is my way of doing it, but there are other ways. Find a room where you can be alone, where no one can interrupt you. For me, this is the bathroom. Clear out this room of any reading material, or anything that might attract attention or something you might be tempted to use if you get bored. Take out the toys, interesting figurines, or stuff like that. Finally, turn off notifications on your phone and other devices. Make sure these devices are not in your room. Then stay or lock yourself in this room shutting out the world for about fifteen minutes. If you must, ask a trusted friend to stand near the door to hold you accountable until time is up. You can do this if you don't trust yourself to follow through. So far, so good.

A few things you should not do once you are in this protected room, don't partake in any strenuous physical activity such as stationary jogging or push-ups. Do not pray; do not speak much at all. Just let yourself do nothing. You are likely to feel very anxious at first if you aren't used to not having something to do. You might even think you hear a phantom notification from your phone or computer. Let yourself feel this slight anxiety. Just let it happen, do nothing. Now just listen and sit there. You will notice your mind starts to become more active, there are new thoughts rushing in, things you have never thought about before, or buried memories. You might begin by thinking about things that bother you, and strangely see some of these things more clearly when making the connection in this moment. You might even have completely new ideas come to you.

This might be followed by feelings of joy, passion, and motivation to act. This is a sign that God is speaking to you. You have allowed yourself to be porous and receive from him, so you hear him. These thoughts might feel intrusive, sharp, and sometimes loud, don't falter just listen. Congratulations, you have learned how to listen to God. Other ideas that can serve the same purpose is taking a walk in the more silent hours. This may be at night or very early in the morning. Do this alone, with no conversation, and no electronic companions.

Listen for the Right Thing

Sometimes people allow themselves to be bored and go through the process only to claim they didn't hear anything. Sometimes it might indeed take more than one occasion before you get anything from God. I find that most times, when people don't hear anything is because they are ignoring what they are already being told. In their minds, they have very specific expectations about what they look forward to hearing. There is nothing wrong with that because sometimes God speaks to that. Sometimes, it might not be the perfect time for the thing that you are most concerned about. God might have other ideas for you. Ideas that are judged to be more important. So, God speaks to you about other things, but you refuse to listen to that because you are focused on something else. This doesn't only apply to moments when you allow yourself to be bored. It applies to any moment. Allow yourself to be open to anything God might be saying even if that thing isn't quite the most important thing to you at that point.

Scanning

What you can do is pray about a particular question, let that sit in your mind, and go about your day. Usually, God will reach out to you about that particular issue in one of the ways we have talked about. Just scan your surroundings and your mind. My favorite way of using this technique is by allowing the question to percolate in my head and then read scripture. It won't be long until I get an "ah-ha!" moment or scripture speaks to my question, or helps shed some light on it.

Consult Other Believers

If you have questions, listen to what the believers around you are saying about the matter. Remember that God can use them to communicate with you. And if what they say is the right thing you will know it in your heart, your soul will resonate. Not only will this be the case, but it will also line up with what you have learned about in scripture.

Pray for Answers

You can pray for answers before bed and hope that God will speak to it in your dreams, sometimes he won't, sometimes he will. Sometimes God has already answered you, and you have to look closely around you, consult his word, spend intimate time with him and open yourself up to hear him.

What you can also do is do what I call a listening prayer. You ask God a question, like "What should I study?" And then you wait, waiting for thoughts in your head to appear, to be filled with ideas and information regarding the topic. God will put ideas and thoughts in your head to answer those questions. It is usually the most random ones, the ones that are more difficult to shake, ignore, or forget. The more commanding they are, the more confident you can be that you are hearing God.

> *"Call to me and I will answer you, and will tell you great and hidden things that you have not known."* - **Jeremiah 33:3**

Make Observations

Words matter, they matter a lot, that is why we watch what we say. But we all know that actions speak louder than words. Sometimes what is real is a far stronger message than what you are hearing. Circumstances, situations, and reality are far more powerful and affecting than flowery, dressed up language. One of the best ways to hear what he is saying is by looking at where you are, what he is doing, and what your options are. Sometimes words won't do; God knows this, and your situation will reveal to you what God's will is, or what he is trying to tell you. This can range from something small to something big. If you have reservations about living in a particular city. Then suddenly, a once in a lifetime opportunity appears there, maybe a position opens up in another company that suits you better. This might be how God is speaking to you, especially if you find you can carry on your faith there. There are measures in place to safeguard it. God might be telling you it is time to move on and cultivate new experiences. Sometimes he speaks to us by taking away options. Things don't quite turn out the way we want so that we may start down a path more suited for us, a path of greater growth and happiness.

Nobody knows why God does this, but he does it. I believe that sometimes God knows the things we are not ready to think about or understand. And we just have to do them. When this happens, your response should be to trust. Trust that whatever is happening is for the best. Because in the end, it always is, even if it takes a while before you realize this.

You should always trust that God is communicating and working hard to help you.

Chapter 2

Purpose

My nephew has a strange question that he likes to ask about specific wildlife. I never ask him why he does this because I never give him a satisfying answer, but he keeps asking anyway. The question is: "What is this for?" Now it would make some sense if he was asking this about tools or toys or something like that. But in each situation, he only wants to know about the animals. As such an odd question, it stays in my mind and I think about it anytime I see a strange creature on TV or online. But I think the question my nephew asks comes intuitively to adults. We are used to things fitting into a category or playing a role. And when I think that way, asking what things are for is no different from asking what they do. The reason why this question stuck with me is that it hints at the deeper question of purpose. Our purpose is the role we play in the grand scheme of things. It is the thing we should be doing with our life. It is the grandest of goals. All your goals or actions in some way, big or small, are in service to this larger mission.

Think of someone making a hammer. What are they making it for? They make it for a purpose. One purpose is to put nails in place, but this tool is multifunctional with many different versions. Not all hammers are made equal, for the same purpose, or used for one thing. Sledgehammers bring down walls and you wouldn't use it to pin a nail. Some hammers are used for smaller tasks like making birdhouses, some are heavier and would come in handy when building a treehouse. Other hammers are just right to use as a paperweight, or their owners use as doorstops. Some hammers come with extra features that allow them to take out nails; some are round enough you can use them to grind grain.

The person making a hammer may have a generic reason behind making it. But hammers are bought with a specific task or several tasks in mind. Their owners give them purpose within this larger set of activities. A hammer is a hammer because of what it does and its features. Not surprisingly, so are people. It may seem strange to talk about humanity in this way because surely, we weren't made for something. People, as a whole, not individuals, were made for the sake of it because it is good. But God has a use for us in his kingdom. He shapes each one of us in a way that serves some purpose because he creates us; he gives us mission, meaning, a point because he has called us to him.

Why Does It Matter?

Humor me for a moment. You are sitting in your living room minding your own business, you have your feet out, nestled in the soft furry carpet or propped up. You like how the carpet feels between your toes and under your feet, it is an enjoyable moment. Now, imagine I come in stomping while wearing shoes with hard soles or heels, and step on your toe. You look at me in pain, a bit confused. But I don't move my foot. I press hard, glaring at you. You could yank your foot back, but you are afraid that you might hurt yourself even more by tearing your skin. The sole of the shoe doesn't feel that smooth. I keep pressing. You could kick me off or push back, but there is something about that glare that makes you think you shouldn't. Now, why does it matter if I am inflicting such pain on you? If I ask you why I should take my foot off, what would your response be?

Think carefully before you answer this question. Don't say something obvious. Clearly, from your groaning and moaning and your disfigured face, you must be in a great deal of pain. So, don't tell me that. Think. Oh, did you just say because it is a nice thing to do? How about how nice it feels to hurt you? That can be nice too. Why does it matter if it's nice or the right thing to do?

If I were to do that and ask for real answers, you wouldn't be able to come up with one satisfying enough. This is because some things just are. I should take my foot off because it hurts; there is no other reason necessary. Also, because it is nice, being nice is good and there is no reason except that it is just the way it is.

Purpose matters because it is nice, and it hurts feeling like you have no purpose. That is just the way it is. People who demand a better answer than that are never successful. But still, people appreciate the exercise, fleshing it out and twirling big concepts in their minds. There is nothing wrong with that. But in the end, it will all circle back to one answer, it hurts not to, and it is good to have a purpose. You don't believe me? Let's toss around the concept of purpose for a while and see where we end up after a few lines.

When we don't have a purpose, we lose our sense of direction. We do not know why we do what we are doing, why it matters, or why we should care a lot about it. You can see just from that set of problems that it is bad. Oops! We're back there again, aren't we? We go back to talk about how feeling like you have direction, meaning and that you matter is nice. See? I can try to come up with other explanations, but they all come back here. Should we give it another try? Okay. A life without purpose is empty, and – no, I can't do it. Sorry, not sorry.

Finding your purpose matters on a cosmic scale because it fulfills a role in the larger divine realm that far supersedes anything we know about the world. Maybe that is why where this strong feeling comes from, from the fact that they are about the best thing that anyone can do in the entire universe, a reason and significance that transcends everything we know and understand. We can speculate about this forever, So I won't spend any time here. In the next section, we talk about how we can find your purpose, God's desire for your life, or his will.

The bottom line is this. We want to know what our purpose is in the world because purpose gives our life meaning and makes us feel fulfilled. The formula is simple, purpose equates to happiness, both earthly happiness and divine happiness. It is the thing that completes us.

Here's How You Know

One way you can find out what is God's purpose for you is to look at your design. Earlier, we talked about hammers and how particular types of hammers are made with a specific purpose in mind. With people, it is like that. We have a collection of traits, abilities, and talents, and these are an indication of what roles we are meant to play. They tell us what our mission is or should be. I can imagine some of you reading this, someone with a misstep between what they are good at and what they are passionate about. I can relate to that. In school, I was very good at science and I was asked by one teacher to join an extracurricular activity involving a science team competing in expos. While I enjoyed traveling and being part of a team, I didn't enjoy these activities very much. With science, I always felt insecure, inadequate, and anxious. But when I was with my fellow nerds, I felt fine. I liked the social side of these events, not the actual science, and I knew it.

Continuing with this logic, it may appear that I was meant to do science, at least something science-related or STEM. I can see that if I had gone down that road and stayed the course long enough maybe I would have found success, but I would have been miserable, as I was most of the time in school. If this was my purpose in life, it sure wasn't pleasant and didn't make me feel passion. I didn't feel I was contributing to something bigger than me, and if I had, I wouldn't have thought it was because I deeply care about it.

Consider another possibility. Sometimes you are passionate about something that you are not good at. Sometimes, although it might be something you were meant to do, you are so horrible at it, and you never seem to advance. Just because you are passionate about one thing, or good at something else, it doesn't automatically mean it is your purpose. But a lot of the time, our purpose is aligned with our passions, with what we are reasonably good at and experience as a defining moment.

Your first clue to what God is saying about your life is both the things you can do and the things you are passionate about. It is this intersection where your purpose lies. Opportunities where these two things come together, are a sign of God calling to you. So, you look at yourself and your personality, and look around you for things that are molded in your shape, these things are what you should be doing. It is in the design.

"The Lord has made everything for its purpose, even the wicked for the day of trouble." **- Proverbs 16:4**

"For we are his workmanship, created in Christ Jesus for good works, which God prepared beforehand, that we should walk in them" **- Ephesians 2:10**

Another way to find out what God wants to do with your life is to listen to what other people around you are saying or what they have said or suggested in the past. Going back to my years as a student, I was told to look towards science as a career and encouraged to do so. If everyone was saying this, this might have meant this is something I should look at closely, something I should work hard to find my passion in because clearly, God wants it for me. But only my science teachers were the ones who thought this. Everyone else saw something different. They talked about my sharp intellect, clear thinking, my beautiful speaking ability, and how I was able to form interesting concepts. They didn't know what I could do with it, but when I found God and started talking about God, this felt right to me and to them too. This group of people was much broader and diverse, not coming from the same teachers, social circle, or school.

This way of looking at things can work for you too. Listen to what different people have always said about you. These people should know you well enough to have valid points about the matter at hand. They shouldn't be people who know little about the subject at hand, or about you or people whose interests are aligned in such a way that they might not be honest with you.

Sometimes God talks to you directly. You begin to hear his voice telling you what you need to do. This way won't be the most common, but it happens if you listen closely and immerse yourself in the word of the Lord. Doing so makes you sensitive to his voice. And when you are that sensitive, God communicates easily about what the next goal in your life should be, or what you should dedicate your life to.

What You Should Do Before Listening

We have talked about yearning for purpose and direction about your life and how it can be communicated to you and how to find it. But you also need to know about the steps you should take so that this revelation comes to you.

The first step you should take should be to clear out the way. Sometimes we can't hear what God desires or is saying about the direction our life should go because we are just too busy building a life we want. We are so hard set on the things we want. We don't stop to listen to what God might want from us. This is the equivalent to pressing mute on God because although we might yearn for him to guide us and point us in a direction, we are only willing to hear it if it lines up in some way with what we want. The noise of our lives, our desires, crowds out God. So, the first step, which is a very difficult one, is to put our desires and wants aside. It is to be willing to reassess and head over in a different direction altogether.

I want you to take a moment to look at your plans for the future, the things you hope to see happen. Now, are you willing to change all of that if God asked you to, or are you so attached to these desires that you might find it difficult to give them up? How about the life you are living now, your job and your lifestyle? Are you willing to change these things? If the answer is no, it might be harder for you to hear what God wants for your life because you have already decided what you want for your life, and you are clearly committed to it. Now that you are committed, find a way to be happy with it. God is not in the business of pushing people to act the way he wants. He likes it if you have a choice in the matter and values autonomy.

"For I know the plans I have for you, declares the Lord, plans for welfare and not for evil, to give you a future and a hope." - **Jeremiah 29:11**

"Many are the plans in the mind of a man, but it is the purpose of the Lord that will

stand." - **Proverbs 19:21**

The way to put your heart in the right place is by realizing that all these plans, desires, the life you lead now are not where purpose and meaning reside. Purpose and meaning reside with God; whatever sense of satisfaction you get from all these other things is nothing compared to what God desires for you. Secondly, all things in life are transient, but it is God's will that is eternal, there is nothing better, more wholesome or complete than putting your life in the hands of God. It is the grandest of endeavors you will ever experience. Who would want anything less? Thirdly, God does not want you to be miserable, so you should be open to his idea, even the very idea that you might need to change your life considerably. He does not promise the process won't be difficult or hard at times, but he guarantees that you will be fulfilled doing it, and you will have a purpose in your life.

Now, it is time to accept God's help in your life. Be willing to lay down your life for him, if you can't do so simply, work at it. One way of doing so is by starting small. That is what the next chapter will explore.

Chapter 3

Day to Day

Here is something you probably already know, but it's worth saying anyway. Big things are made up of smaller things. Life is also made of sets of little decisions and events that add up to something bigger than the sum of its parts. Involving God in your day-to-day activities, even on the smallest scale, works to infuse the very fabric of your life with his presence. We need to feel God's presence in our lives, get accustomed to it and who he is to us; this will make it easier for us to trust him with the rest of our lives. Maybe all we need to do is just trust him with the small things, and those small things make a life.

The Small Things Matter

When looking at your day, it is composed of small transient decisions that you don't spend a lot of time thinking about. You wake up and decide to shower or skip it; if you should make breakfast or grab a pastry on the way; if you should wear one particular outfit instead of another. Then when you leave your house, if you should take one street or go the back way depending on known traffic delays so you can get to work on time. Or if you should have a second cup of coffee or drink more water. Our days are filled with these little insignificant decisions. You might think of these as little detours in an otherwise busy day filled with activity, but I have news for you: They make up a good portion of your day, time-wise. And way more than you think.

If you had to split your hours for a day, they would account for more than a third of that time. I realized this when I downloaded an activity tracking app on my phone that also linked to my laptop. It would note any and all movement throughout the day, and it also kept track of which apps I was using and how much 'screen time' I was using. At the end of the day, I would have a comprehensive grouping of information on how I spent my time. There would always be a huge chunk of time that went unallocated. From this report you would say I spend more time playing than putting in actual work hours. This was a surprise because in my mind I thought I spent a lot of time being productive with my work or work-related tasks and I do, but not as much as I originally thought.

The missing time was made up of those little unavoidable things. Little things that have nothing to do with being productive or having fun, they are what happens in between work and play. The bad part is you don't really notice how much time they take up in your day and add up to make up for a good portion of your life. Like when you see statistics online for how much of your life you spend in traffic on your daily commute or how much your life consists of sleeping. But you rarely see any numbers on decision making, or small menial tasks that are neither work nor play.

Let's talk about play. Play is made up of these little decisions that take up a lot of time. I choose these areas because they are the ones that most people are themselves when they do, offering a great deal of freedom. If you invite God into these areas of your life, you give God a large share of your life. The good part is that you don't have to do anything drastic, you just have to let him choose which movie or show you should watch, or to read instead, if you should have sugar with your coffee, or take a walk in the neighborhood. In this way, you are getting acquainted with the spirit of God. You normalize his presence and his ways and soon learn to trust him. And when you trust him, it will be easy for you to start listening when he tells you something about your life. God will also entrust you with bigger things if you have shown your faith in the small stuff.

Here are just a few examples of the small stuff, yours will look different than mine and make it your own by adding more to the list because it is meant to be extensive.

- What you should watch.
- What you should eat.
- What you should drink.
- What you should do with your leisure time.
- What books you should read.
- Where you should spend your time on social media and how long.
- Should you get a pet or a plant?
- What should you do for physical activity?
- Should you take a nap?
- Should you be drinking more water?

- Should you engage in small talk with that woman from work every day?
- Should you say hi to your neighbor?

How to Listen

I apologize if I make it sound like you should always pray, close your eyes, wait for God to answer every time and want an extra slice of toast. Well, no, that is not a very practical way to live, and in fact, it might cause you more problems than ever bringing you closer to God. Living a life where you are always waiting for an answer from God, for him to weigh in every little decision will not work out the way you want. But God does have input on many of the small things we do every day. So, what is he saying to you, and how do you hear him?

Nagging

The truth is most people don't hear what God is saying about their everyday decisions because they don't like what he is saying, or they are too busy avoiding or assuming he never speaks or never speaks to them specifically. God has already spoken about something in your life. You're probably waiting for him to say something else, or something new, but he won't say any more than he already has said if you are not listening.

You know that voice in your head that tells you maybe you shouldn't have another donut, or another glass of wine, or you should watch how much sugar you take each day and start answering your mom's phone call? That might actually be God talking to you. Because of how often this voice is with us, telling us what we should and shouldn't do and making us feel bad when we do something we know we aren't supposed to, I call it the 'nagging'. It's as if someone is standing behind you, nagging you to do something. Sometimes people are so set on an objective that hearing this voice has little to no effect at all on their decision. They have given up on feelings of remorse if it doesn't affect them.

Sometimes this voice is just our subconscious, compiling the past, present, and dreams of the future putting together appropriate thoughts and ways we can behave, guiding our behavior to reach assorted goals. It is our self-policing voice. When it is God using this voice, there are a few signs. What the voice has told you is often in the back of your head; it lingers there no matter what you are doing. It convicts you, and it bothers you. It is the same feeling you get when a picture on your wall is hanging crooked, and you can't resist the urge to set it straight. Except in this situation, it is this feeling and this voice about something you are doing or should do, but unlike the crooked picture in your hallway, it is usually something you find daunting to do. So, you put it off, the longer you put it off, the more desensitized you become to this sensation.

If you want God in your life, you should start by listening to what he says about the little things in your present day situation. Start with something simple; do the bare minimum if you have to. But whatever that thing is, do it now, and you will notice God speaking to other areas of your life, and it will be easier to trust him. You will find that you become a lot lighter and happy with yourself. It's like putting on glasses for the first time. You never quite know how bad your vision is before putting on prescription lenses. You don't know how tense, miserable, or out of balance you are until you start listening to that voice.

I have made it sound like this voice will only talk to you about do's and don'ts. Sometimes this voice brings about ideas, too, it brings passion and inspiration. You know it is from God when it lines up with scripture, is constructive instead of destructive, and it adds a sense of direction to your life. When you show your faith in this area of your life, God will start opening doors for you and speaking to you about things that are life-defining; because small things make up big things.

"Do not be anxious about anything, but in everything by prayer and supplication with thanksgiving let your requests be made known to God. And the peace of God, which surpasses all understanding, will guard your hearts and your minds in Christ Jesus."
- Philippians 4:6-7

Reading Scripture

Make it a habit to start each day by reading scripture, even if it is a few lines or a paragraph, meditate on it and think about its application to your life and relevance. If in some way it connects or speaks to your situation you will spot little things you can start doing differently on that day. Sometimes ideas will come, and other times there will be nothing. The best part is that no line can go to waste; one day in some other situation, these words will come to the forefront of your mind and guide you.

"My sheep hear my voice, and I know them, and they follow me. I give them eternal life, and they will never perish, and no one will snatch them out of my hand."

- **John 10:27-28**

Chapter 4

Light of Darkness

In the introduction, I mentioned the spirit world being abundant, and how some of them may want to influence you in some ways. I gave you a reason to prefer God, above all else. But you might have wondered how you will know if these are bad spirits trying to speak and make a connection with you. How can you have eyes that look out in the world and easily pick out the good from the bad? I will answer this question at the end of this chapter. First, I feel I have to explain terms like the spiritual world/realm and the spirits themselves. I am not going into demonology here, think of it as metaphysics.

Nature of Spirits

First let's get one thing out of the way: The thought that the spiritual world is a place inhabited by all things spiritual is misleading because it gives the idea that the physical world and the spiritual world are separate. Like I said, spirits and spiritual things mingle with and live within the same universe created by God. They are phenomena that we don't observe directly with our mind or tools, but since it exists within this universe, it interacts with and can influence our observable experience. It is a bit like we have spiritual blindness, spiritual things exist and interact with us every day, but we have a hard time perceiving them.

Spirits are consciousness that exist away from our direct observation. Because they have desires, they like and dislike just the same. Think about humanity and imagine that we were largely invisible to creatures who we share the world with. Imagine they couldn't see us, but could sometimes sense us, that we could influence their events and themselves to achieve a state of affairs that is most desirable to our desires. That is what spirits are. There is something else too, like how other species interact with others, there is a bit of speciesism going on. They act on self-interest, often at the detriment of humans, our wellbeing and success. This is because it is much better for them this way. Some people like to think of spirits as unreasonably bad to humans. It may very well be that they are. But think of how humans are bad to other species for our own good. Spirits don't need us; unlike us, we need our environment, but spirits treat us the way they do because of their interests, ruthless because they think of themselves as superior, deserving of more. Sounds familiar?

> *"Be sober-minded; be watchful. Your adversary the devil prowls around like a roaring lion, seeking someone to devour."* **- 1 Peter 5:8**

God and his pals, the angels, are the ones saying we are special, and they want to protect us and all that. The other guys are maddened by this, perhaps filled with jealousy because of it. So, they want to sabotage us for this reason and others unbeknown to us, the reason that has to do with their wants and interests separate from envy and anger. When you are not with God, you open yourself up to a lot of other spirits, whose interest doesn't necessarily align with yours, they have little to no reason to care about your well-being. But God does.

"For I am sure that neither death nor life, nor angels nor rulers, nor things present nor things to come, nor powers, nor height nor depth, nor anything else in all creation, will be able to separate us from the love of God in Christ Jesus our Lord." - **Romans 8:38-39**

Here's How You Know

I have given away how you can tell if a bad spirit is trying to connect with you. The ways I will discuss here relate to that element of self-interest in the expanse of people.

Spirits speak to us a lot through negative talk. They attack us at the very core. This is often seen in how they make people think that they are selfish, undeserving, or just bad. They breed and maintain a state of mind and perception that sell the story that human beings are terrible, or you as an individual are bad, unclean, unlovable or incapable. They breed low self-esteem, doubt, anxiety, and distorted self-images. If we can't find love for ourselves in our minds, the natural thing is to neglect ourselves and even harm ourselves, and we do so through acts that are detrimental to our wellbeing. We may abuse alcohol. We may act in ways that destroy our relationships, refrain from taking on opportunities because we are too afraid. We may even put off doing work because we feel ill-equipped. All these acts stem from a deep-seated sense of inadequacy. If you have persistent thoughts in your head that contribute to these feelings, you have a bad spirit in your hands. It's even worse if the spirit has you convinced that it is God.

Here are some examples of ways this spirit will speak to you:

1. "You are a nobody."
2. "Nobody cares about you."
3. "You are worthless."
4. "You can't do anything right."
5. "You are a sinner, and a hypocrite. That is why you keep having these dirty thoughts."
6. "Things will never work out. Everything always falls apart."
7. "You really thought you could do that? Have you looked at yourself?"
8. "You are a loser and a failure."
9. "Everything you touch fails, stay away!"

These types of thoughts will hijack your normal sense of guilt if you do something wrong. They exaggerate and embolden your guilt to such an extent that is overwhelming and morphs into feelings of inadequacy and highlights your imperfections. God would never torture you about your mistakes. He wouldn't spend every minute of the day telling you are unworthy just because of a passing sultry thought about a colleague. He expects you to acknowledge what you did was wrong, but to also move on from it, and he will work quickly on making sure this happens. If it means that you should forgive yourself, give yourself a slight slap on the wrist and laugh about it, good! Being miserable about it is a sure way to get yourself dragged into more sin. So, if you are driven to a point where you can't forgive yourself, you might have a spirit on your hands, tormenting you. God works to heal you, and self- forgiveness is an important step in that process.

"There is therefore now no condemnation for those who are in Christ Jesus."
- Romans 8:1

"If we confess our sins, he is faithful and just to forgive us our sins and to cleanse us from all unrighteousness." **- 1 John 1:9**

But wait, what if you actually are a bad guitar player, or learning a new language? Then this can't just be some spirit trying to hurt you, right? In other words, what if you are making a good personal judgment about your abilities or traits and this observation is somewhat uncomfortable to admit or painful to think about. For me, it was when I had to come to terms with the fact that perhaps I wasn't the best singer, even after all the while thinking I was. And that I am really bad at cooking. These are what I call objective judgments, and they are different from negative talk in many ways.

If you are convinced of a truth about yourself that is not actually true, you might already be suffering from that inability to appreciate your reality. Objective judgments work well for us because they are freeing. They free us from problems of self-delusion. Objective judgments feel more like a weight being lifted off your shoulders, although at first, they might create some pain and discomfort. This is normal because you are adjusting to a new reality while letting go of something you invested a lot into. Negative self-talk does the opposite. It brings more misery, confusion, and it actually makes us more blind and disconnected from our reality.

How do you see it in other people, how do you know they are under the influence of bad spirits or if they harbor bad intentions against you? The way to discern this is by paying attention to your underlying emotions or gut feelings. The spirit speaks to us about others this way. The spirit of God can perceive what we cannot, and if something is off, it will communicate this, and it is up to us to listen and act accordingly. How many times have you heard someone say, "I knew there was something with that guy" or "I totally saw it coming, I don't know why I didn't say something"? Probably a lot. In these cases, it might have been the spirit telling you about something it can see, and you cannot. So, listen closely to that feeling whenever you interact with others.

So, what if you are often very gullible believing whatever you are told? Seek the counsel of others who are acquainted with God and the spirit in the way that you are, they might be more attuned to what God is saying then you are. Here is a safe place where your suspicions can be confirmed or corrected.

Positive Talk

So, when is positive talk good? We are constantly told to be positive and allow only positive things in, but we just now established that this is not always a good idea. We should be vigilant of the influences we let in even when they are nice sounding. Positive talk is good when it is not binding to the things in your situations that need you to work at. God has probably been talking to you about those things in your life and how you should work on them, you do the difficult thing of being honest and hearing that deeper voice in you that is telling you about the flawed thing in your life. Good positive talk does not feel dirty. There is a sense in the back of your head or elsewhere that makes you feel bad, anxious, or confused.

We all have bad, positive talk voices in our heads. Mine tells me I am the right weight for my height. But when I calculated my BMI, it shows I am in the overweight range for my age and height. I looked at myself in the mirror and said, "What now?" The voice in my head says, "You still aren't as fat as your friend Mary or cousin Katie. So, it's not that bad," even though it is. Other people's challenges don't make mine any less meaningful; this voice in place is a distraction. So instead of agreeing with this voice, I took steps to fix my problem. I started watching my diet, and how many hours I was active a day.

Think about the gambler who loses his life savings and still thinks if he bets on this horse or draws one more time, he could make the money back? That may seem like a positive outlook on life, but it is not helpful, it is harmful. Chances are the gambler who will lose all his money will put him in debt, miserable, and maybe even without a home. It comes in other forms too, like denying that you are addicted to a substance. You have heard this before, "I can quit anytime. I don't need it." This can be reassuring to the person who says that it just makes them feel good, invincible, or superior, but this is a trap to lure them into complacency and a state of ignorance until it is too late and the substance has caused them a great amount of pain or loss. Think about the student who looks at her mid-term grades and says, "It's not that bad. I can make it up." We love when people stay positive and are motivated to achieve their goals and overcome great odds. But ideally, we don't want to live in a world where people have to overcome the odds to achieve something that doesn't need to cost that much to achieve. This is why we want to avoid it because we know that most of the time, attempting the unlikely leads to failure.

One of the blatant ways that spirits attack us is through negative talk. It is so very easy to recognize that for some of you, you wonder why I even mentioned it at all. Well, I've got to cover my bases. By the most insidious one I find is positive talk, which sometimes takes the veil of denial or lying. We have quickly mentioned how self-delusions can cause a lot of pain; this is like that but not always like that.

Separate Bad Things from Evil

Evil spirits work in your life by making bad things happen. A lot of bad things can happen to you, but there are broadly two types, those that are a result of nature and those that happen because of evil spirits. The trick is being able to distinguish between the two.

Terrible things, as a result of nature, can be harmful and traumatic—like death and natural disaster. Another type is accidents that happen because of human failings or human error. People are not perfect; they make mistakes, and sometimes these mistakes lead to very sad outcomes. These are car accidents, an explosion at a chemical plant, or a partnership ending in divorce. The way we know these events are as a result of how the world is or of how we are, they aren't intent on destroying our faith, distancing us from God. Yes, they may be depressing, but they won't taunt us to abandon God or our faith. They also won't make us feel extraordinarily stuck. Our efforts to overcome a bad situation will feel successful, even when it happens in a very slow way. Don't feel stuck. These situations might demand a great deal of patience to overcome, and we will see this because our efforts count towards something. You may give up, but you will know it is not because things are fundamentally broken or not working.

Bad things that happen as a result of bad spirits will challenge your faith. They attack, taunting you to give it up, just like the story of Job. You will notice in this story that the more faithful Job becomes, the worse the situation becomes, and he is constantly being challenged to give up his faith in God. When you face a challenge that hacks at the core of faith, and when you try to be faithful and read the bible or go to church, these activities feel very difficult. It might be an evil spirit attacking you. You shouldn't feel like the thing is getting worse the more you turn to God; you should be filled with hope and a sense of working towards a desirable end. Now, things might turn out badly, your spouse might die from a terminal illness, but it is the desirable end in the grand scheme of things. You shouldn't feel stuck, trapped, or completely out of control. You shouldn't feel alone or abandoned by God. If you feel this way, you might have a spirit on your hands.

People Under the Influence of Spirits

If you can be that kind to yourself, you should be that way with other people. Bad spirits form entire world views, ways of thinking that can make people act against their interest. Spirits are more clever than we are, they see more, they need to possess people to be effective. They just need to nudge things the right way.

You will meet people in your life that are not good for you. Some of them are just flawed humans, and others are under the influence of a bad spirit. Now, I don't mean possession. I am not going to tell you that your annoying neighbor is trying your faith because they are possessed. Talking about possession or using it as an excuse for foul behavior dehumanizes people, and demonizes them. And once you demonize people, it becomes very difficult to find love or understand them in your heart. And when you find it difficult to find love or understanding in your heart for others, you are not listening to the spirit of God. People that are influenced by spirits to do certain things are the same as you. You are just as vulnerable to bad influence if you don't examine yourself carefully. You can't say to me, honestly, that there isn't an area in your life where you feel challenged, or you struggle because of your weaknesses, and there aren't spiritual entities trying to exploit that and often succeed. Sometimes spirits don't need to say anything. They just need to crowd your environment and create a situation that challenges your faith and make you falter. And if/when you do, don't be hard on yourself, the goal is to grow intimacy with God not to chastise yourself for every mistake you make.

People in your life under the influence of spirits will work to undermine your faith and relationship with God in the things they do directly and indirectly. I want to emphasize that people who do this are not evil, it might be comforting for you to think that they are this way, but it is simply not true. It is the kind of thinking that takes away your love for others and makes enemies of people who are victims. These people don't really hate you; they might have hate in them, but it comes from a largely ill-advised place. So, your response should be that of compassion and try to help them or get yourself out of the web spun around you.

When you begin to tease out the light from the darkness, be careful of the following emotions and thoughts. I want to list them here and make it easy to remember.

- Judging other people.
- Thinking people are evil or possessed.
- Despising others or feeling a strong sense of dislike or hatred.
- Thinking the world might be better off without certain people instead of others.
- Harboring anger for those who protect harmful ideas and ways of living.

- Being tempted to take drastic measures bordering on immoral or illegal acts to protect yourself.
- Closing yourself off to other people when they explain to you their experience or reality.
- Trying to enforce your way of seeing things on others.

You should watch out for these things because they drive you back to the swamp that you are trying to clear. Instead of fixing things and advancing God, you are recruiting yourself into the auxiliary forces of the enemy. And these spirits like this type of soldier, the one who thinks they are on the right side because they do the work for them without even realizing it and they also demonize fellow believers sowing discord.

Chapter 5

Wisdom

In the introduction, I briefly touched on wisdom without openly mentioning it. People often conflate wisdom with knowledge and intelligence. Wisdom is about the optimum application of tools like knowledge, intelligence, and talent. The big question is, how do you obtain wisdom? Wisdom is such an ill-understood but a widely desired attribute among believers. They think it has a lot of benefits, and it is true it is. God wouldn't want it for us if it were for nothing.

What It Is

Wisdom is a much broader meaning of what discernment is. Discernment concerns itself with the spiritual world over the readily experienced world. It is about being spiritually perceptive while going about your life and in the world and develops after establishing an intimate relationship with God. This relationship will serve to sharpen your spiritual instincts that you may walk out into the word with little that passes by you. This is why the emphasis of this book has been on communication with God. It is the fertile ground form in which discernment grows.

Wisdom is about how the knowledge you have, both the things life teaches you and formal education, come into action in your life, especially in matters that have little to do with spirituality. This is a fine distinction, one that doesn't hold to powerful scrutiny. It is essentially the story of how the experience makes us more adept in our dealings, both spiritual and not.

God's Wisdom in Action

When you are filled with God's wisdom, you grow in confidence, peace, and conform to the decisions you make. Your decisions and how you go about in the world promote love, peace, they shun all prejudice, and advance God's kingdom. Your undertakings in the world are done through patience, from a position of empathy, sympathy, and humility.

It is difficult to explain wisdom, but there is an analogy. Before you start your relationship with God, you have had world experiences, and they make up your worldly wisdom. You are like a crudely shaped hunk of marble, sharp edges, rough surfaces, and ungainly curves. You are something, but not quite it. When you get to God, he whips out his hammer and chisel, and he knocks off some of the unwanted stone, he might remove entire curves altogether. You might look misshapen at first, but he soon gets to work creating new shapes and curves. He gives you a striking form and a new shape. He smoothens out the edges, surfaces, and the curves bringing out a god/goddess.

Through his relationship, you become endowed with traits and features whose application is wisdom.

- Knowing when to quit or work harder.
- Knowing when making a deal is best.

- Having foresight.
- Having sensibility for appropriateness.
- Going through difficulties and still retaining a spirit of calm.
- When you have an acute awareness of your abilities and know how to apply them.
- You are about the outcomes of your whole life, not just yourself.
- Your instincts are to seek cooperation not competition.
- You value knowledge for its sake, not what it can do for you.
- You realize there are no such things as time lost.
- You know how to listen and hear exactly what others are saying.
- You come to appreciate the power of observation.
- You don't get into debates to win; you seek to learn something new and correct your mistakes.
- You aren't ashamed of your mistakes and flaws to the point of inaction. You recognize that everyone has them too, the wise thing is to move forward.
- You value consistency over sudden flashes of genius.
- You are not scared of your mortality.
- You realize judging others is fruitless.

There are many other traits out there that are the mark of wisdom. You will know them when you see them.

"But the fruit of the Spirit is love, joy, peace, patience, kindness, goodness, faithfulness, gentleness, self-control; against such things there is no law."

- Galatians 5:22-23

Conclusion

"And when he had said these things, he knelt down and prayed with them all. And there was much weeping on the part of all; they embraced Paul and kissed him, being sorrowful most of all because of the word he had spoken, that they would not see his face again. And they accompanied him to the ship." - **Acts 20:36-38**

With this text we have done a lot for ourselves. I started off by talking about the typical ways that God speaks. Then I showed you how you could know it is God speaking. I also shared some tips about how to listen to him when he speaks. Realizing that this information could be limited. I created two chapters that deal with purpose and everyday living. These chapters are related because small things make big things. We talked about giving god charge of the little things, he may trust you with the bigger things. We also acknowledged this would make you more comfortable with God taking over, for those who were a bit reluctant to relinquish control over. I hope this can be spread to those you care about, and with active practice, it will.

Even if you stopped reading there, it was a good start, but something was missing. You also needed to understand that there are various influences out there that don't have your best interest at heart. We had to talk about them, learn how to recognize them and how you should treat them when all is said and done. This information helps you see your enemies, externally and within. It also taught you about lapses in thought that make it easy for these influences to upend your life. This was far from the longest of all parts, but it was nice.

The last thing we did was talk about wisdom. More like I showed that if you practice everything we have talked about in this book consistently, you will have it and God will shape you. This is great because we finally understood that wisdom is a process; it isn't a set of instructions.

I am on the porch sipping on tea looking out in the yard, watching the children play about the street and all is calm once more. And I say to you, dear friend, it has been a journey. Thank you for joining me on it.

Bonus!

Wouldn't it be nice to have even more motivation, inspiration and courage on your spiritual path? As a sincere "Thank you" from the bottom of my heart, i've given you access to a FREE powerful 10 minute guided gratitude meditation below. Gratitude is the key to all of your life's abundance, joy, and manifests a wealth of love and light. Practicing the meditation below each day has enriched my life immensely, I just know it will do the same for you.

Are You Searching For The Guidance of God's Higher Power?

- Connect To His Light Easily Through The Power of Gratitude

- Clear The Haze of Uncertainty From Your Life Path

- Discern More Easily Between Bad Spirits & Good

- **Go To This Link For Your FREE 10 Min Guided Meditation Mp3**

bit.ly/spiritualdiscernmentmp3

This meditation often helped me immensely when his exact path for me was not always overtly clear. Resting in gratitude for the beauty I already had in my life cleared the haze & created more of the same. I know these words will help guide you towards your destiny with courage and determination!

Lastly…Please Leave a Review

From the bottom of my heart, thank you for reading my book. I truly hope that it helps you on your spiritual journey and to live a more empowered and happy life. If it does help you, then I'd like to ask you for a favor. Would you be kind enough to leave an honest review for this book on Amazon? It'd be greatly appreciated and will likely impact the lives of other spiritual seekers across the globe, giving them hope and power.

I read **EVERY** review I receive & each one helps me to become a better spiritual teacher so that I can serve you better.

Thank you and good luck!

Angela Grace

www.ingramcontent.com/pod-product-compliance
Lightning Source LLC
Chambersburg PA
CBHW071915070526
44583CB00016B/2001